Publish
Like the Pros

Traditional self-publishing has been hijacked (I should know!). Authors who follow the "do-it-yourself" approach recommended by self-serving POD publishers soon discover that plain covers do not attract buyers. In *Publish Like the Pros: A Brief Guide to Quality Self-Publishing*, Michele DeFilippo explains how quality books have always been created—with an eye to the future. Armed with this advice, authors can take full advantage of today's unprecedented opportunity to distribute and promote their books without middlemen, and successfully compete in the book publishing industry.

—Dan Poynter, author of *The Self-Publishing Manual*

Within 78 pages, Michele DeFilippo packs a lot of information. It's one of those gems that deliver a kick-butt reality check as to *why* every newbie and oldie author needs to step up to the publishing plate and create non-cheesy looking and well written books.

DeFilippo is an insider, she gets a lot of garbage in her studios; when the books exit, they are a total makeover. As the CEO of 1106 Design in Phoenix, AZ, she knows books.

As someone who has seen too many books that should have avoided the RTP Syndrome—Rush to Publish, this is a good one to read through as a quick reminder for your To Do publishing list. Slow it down, get it right and done right. Then, you too, can publish like the pros.

—Judith Briles, author of *Author YOU: Creating and Building Your Author and Book Platforms*

DeFilippo has written a complete overview of the book industry and the publishing process that will allow both authors and self-publishers to make their way through the self-publishing process quickly and successfully. I was amazed at the up-to-date insights and money-saving advice in this book! Want to do it right? Want to avoid a lot of the mistakes that plague first time self-publishers? Read *Publish Like the Pros* and call 1106 Design.

—Amy Collins, owner of New Shelves Distribution,
http://www.newshelves.com

Publish
Like the Pros

A BRIEF GUIDE TO QUALITY SELF-PUBLISHING

{ AND AN **INSIDER'S LOOK** AT A **MISUNDERSTOOD INDUSTRY** }

Michele DeFilippo

1106 design
Traditional Publisher Quality
For Independent Authors

Phoenix, Arizona

Copyrighted Material

Publish Like the Pros: A Brief Guide to Quality Self-Publishing

Copyright © 2021 by 1106 Design, LLC. All rights reserved.

No part of this publication may be reproduced, stored in a retrieval system or transmitted, in any form or by any means—electronic, mechanical, photocopying, recording or otherwise—without prior written permission from the publisher, except for the inclusion of brief quotations in a review.

For information about this title or to order additional books and/or electronic media, contact the publisher:

1106 Design, LLC
E-mail: md@1106design.com
https://1106design.com

ISBNs:
Print: 978-0-9854899-0-8
Kindle and ePub: 978-0-9854899-2-2

Printed in the United States of America

*This book is dedicated
to my parents,
Margaret and John,
to my son, John,
and to my granddaughter, Nora.
You taught me everything
that matters in life.*

Table of Contents

Introduction	1
Chapter One: Before You Start	**5**
The Truth About Self-Publishing	5
Six Steps to a Quality Book	9
So, How Long Does All This Take?	13
How Much of My Time is Required?	13
Experts = An Enjoyable Process and a Better Book	14
Printed Book or eBook? The Parable of the Pumpernickel Baker	14
Chapter Two: About Your Cover	**21**
Your Book's Title	22
Back Cover Copy	23
Cover Design	26
How Authors Can Help Book Designers	27
Getting an ISBN	28
Chapter Three: Editing	**31**
The Importance of Editing	33

Chapter Four: Interior Layout   37
    Why Your Book Layout Needs a
        Professional Touch   37
    What Do Book Designers Really Do?   42
    Get the Most from Your Book Design Dollar   45

Chapter Five: Proofreading   51
    Why You Should Proofread Your Book
        Before Typesetting   51
    Why You Should Proofread Your Book
        After Typesetting   52

Chapter Six: Book Distribution, Pricing and Marketing   55
    Book Distribution   56
    How to Determine Your Book's Price   60
    A Marketing Plan for Your Book   64

Conclusion   73

Acknowledgments   77

About the Author   79

Introduction

IF YOU ARE READING THIS BOOK, then you are considering self-publishing as a way of making your book a reality and putting it into the hands of your readers. Self-publishing is a great choice; there is almost nothing more satisfying than "giving birth" to your own publication. However, self-publishing is a process that is potentially fraught with confusion and pitfalls if you don't understand the process and the players—or choose the right team to work with you.

This book takes a "no holds barred" approach to describing the process of turning your manuscript into a professional book. We take an honest look at the steps involved to self-publish a book and the decisions you must make along the way. We also offer you a "peek" into the self-publishing industry, which will provide you with valuable information that is guaranteed to help you navigate the world of self-publishing.

First, let's make an important clarification regarding print-on-demand (POD) companies and self-publishing. POD printing is an alternative to traditional offset printing, where a set quantity of books are printed and sent to a distributor. POD companies print only enough copies of your book to satisfy immediate orders. They will print and ship the required number of copies to you, a distributor, Amazon, bookstores or customers. Anyone can order POD services; authors can go directly to the POD company and set up their account. It is not necessary to go through a self-publishing company in order to get POD services, although self-publishing companies would have you think otherwise. In fact, many self-publishing companies have gone so far as to merge "self-publishing" and "POD printing" into something called "POD publishing," leading authors to think that the only path to POD is through them, while the truth is they use the same POD companies that you can contact yourself.

It's not necessary (or even advisable) to work with a "POD publisher" or a "self-publishing company" to publish a book, and that's because you, yourSELF, are the publisher. You, yourSELF can, and should, obtain the necessary editing, design, and printing or POD services that best suit your situation. You don't need to purchase the services that a self-publishing or "POD publishing"

Introduction

company will try to sell you, nor do you need to do everything yourself.

Self-publishing does NOT mean that you have to lay out your cover and interior yourself, or ask Aunt Tilly to edit the manuscript because she taught English in 1935. But this is exactly what the POD publishers promote. They don't teach clients how REAL publishers prepare books for market; they lie to make the process sound easy so that everyone will sign up. But it ain't easy. And that's the premise of this book: We will teach you how real publishers prepare books for market so that you can emulate them.

The first thing you need to know about publishing is that it's a lot of hard work. POD publishers may promise you an easy way out with "free" production, easy-to-use templates, promises of assured sales and more. If your book is your hobby, then by all means use a POD publisher; they offer the cheapest way to produce a small quantity of books for friends and family. But if your publishing goals are more substantial, or the purpose of your book is to promote yourself or your business, then it's important to "go pro" right from the start. The good news is that many experts (including 1106 Design) are ready, willing and able to help you craft a quality book. Isn't that what you set out to do in the first place?

So now, as a self-publisher, you are taking the first step: choosing a team of professionals to help you produce your book. The Before You Start chapter of this book will give you some insight to the self-publishing industry and help you define who the "players" are and the pitfalls to avoid. Also in this chapter are the Six Steps to a Quality Book and a parable to help you decide whether to produce an eBook or a printed book. Using the Six Steps as a framework, this book provides you with helpful information about creating a dynamic cover, the importance of editing, why a professional interior book design is crucial, tips on working with your designer, why proofreading should never be skipped, and a list of considerations for your marketing plan.

Marketing plan? Yes. Unless your book is your hobby, you need to treat self-publishing as a business. Hopefully you researched the potential market for your book before you started writing. You should also spend a good amount of time researching and estimating the costs involved in producing the book in various formats. Perhaps this is the step you are at now and we think you will find this book useful in your research.

Again, congratulations on your choice to self-publish your book. As you embark upon this adventure, we think you will find this book informative, and you should feel free to contact us with any questions that you may have.

CHAPTER ONE

Before You Start

NOW THAT YOU'RE A PUBLISHER, you're going to check out the templates on that cool website—the one that promised you could print your book for free, right? Wrong! This chapter takes a hard look at the self-publishing industry, the importance of hiring professionals to turn your hard work into a professional publication, the six steps to transforming your manuscript into a book, and the question of producing your book in electronic format only.

The Truth About Self-Publishing
It has been said that if you tell a lie loud enough or often enough, it begins to sound like the truth.

Publish Like the Pros

Those of us who have worked in publishing for most of our lives—particularly book editors, book designers and typesetters—are about to go mad at the misinformation about self-publishing that today is regurgitated and unfortunately widely accepted.

Let's have a little fun. Pretend that you go to the doctor. She says you need surgery and it's going to cost a lot of money. You leave her office and drive directly to the library to check out a medical textbook. A few moments later, at the medical supply store, you buy a scalpel and a few other supplies. You hand the book and the scalpel to a friend and say, "This is easy. Just hand me that bottle of bourbon and we can do it ourselves. The step-by-step instructions are right there . . . there's nothing to it!"

Sounds crazy, doesn't it? And yet there are many websites that promise uninformed authors that they can self-publish a book—without editing, without design, without quality typesetting—if only they give XYZ Company a little money. XYZ will take care of all the hard work. XYZ will make their book available in bookstores nationwide. XYZ will market their book. Soon, the author will be as famous as Stephen King or Dean Koontz. It's easy. Just upload your Word file, they say, and use our easy cover templates. You don't need experts.

Before You Start

You can do everything yourself—no training, no experience, no talent required.

Self-confidence is an unparalleled source of courage that propels us forward toward a goal when everyone else thinks we're crazy. But really, does it seem sensible to you that anyone's first-time efforts at book editing, design and typesetting will compare to the results that professionals can achieve? Apparently so, judging by the thousands of authors who use these services.

In some cases, people just don't know there's a better way. If you do a Google search on "self-publishing," a good portion of the search results will unfortunately be listings for "self-publishing companies" or "POD publishers," both of which are, in reality, nothing more than vanity presses. If you drill down through several pages, you will discover that there are competent editors, designers, printers, and publicists who offer far better services and results, albeit at a higher cost.

While it may be tempting to use a vanity service that promises to do everything for you at a price you can afford, there are more important numbers to consider, namely book sales. The largest of the so-called "self-publishing companies" report that the average author sells fifty books. Yes, fifty. Selling just fifty books isn't anyone's goal after spending many months or even years on a manuscript.

So what does that tell us? That something is very wrong. And, whether it's welcome news or not, we experts—the ones you'll almost never find in search results—know what that "something" is.

Self-publishing is hard work. As Dan Poynter, The Book Futurist, says, "If you want your book to sell like a book, it has to look like a book." No matter how proud you may be of your own beginner's efforts at editing, typesetting and design, the truth is an amateur job will never be more than an amateur job. That's why reviewers won't even open a book from most of the self-publishing companies. Reviewers and retailers know that these companies don't serve the author; they serve themselves. By allowing anyone to publish anything without any quality control, the self-publishing companies make their money on the front end, not from book sales. Yes, they make their money by selling YOU a fairy tale.

Here's what we experts are shouting from the rooftops to anyone who will listen. Your book needs professional editing, professional cover design, professional typesetting and professional marketing and publicity to stand out in a crowded marketplace. This costs money. There's no way around that. Not if you want a quality book that has the best possible chance to sell. You can believe the fairy tales if you want, but that won't make them true.

Writing a book is an awesome accomplishment. Self-publishing is a steep hill to climb, for anyone. Please, hire pros who can help you create a product that the market will accept.

Six Steps to a Quality Book

When self-publishing was just beginning to take off, 1106 Design's owner, Michele DeFilippo, talked with author Jane Kimball, who had recently learned from a book printer that the services of a book designer were required before her book could be printed.

Thus began 1106 Design's year-long association with Jane to design her masterwork, *Trench Art: An Illustrated History*, a four-hundred-page, full-color book featuring more than one thousand items from her personal collection of war souvenirs. These artifacts, collectively known as "trench art," were meticulously crafted by soldiers from spent shell casings and other materials beginning in World War I.

"I didn't even know there was such a thing as a book designer!" Jane quipped.

"That's alright," Michele replied. "I didn't know there was such a thing as trench art!"

You see, because self-publishing was still fairly new, all of our customers up until that point were seasoned publishers who were familiar with book design and understood what we do. Jane was the first customer to whom we had to explain our services, but she certainly wasn't the last. In subsequent conversations, Jane related to Michele, and other team members, that book design and production is a very scary subject to many first-time authors, who worry that hiring experts will cause them to lose control of their "baby."

What follows is a brief description of a typical book design project that will hopefully put your mind at ease. Far from losing control of your book, you'll actually collaborate closely with experts every step of the way to make your book the very best it can be.

Step 1: Cover Design
The first task in preparing a book for publication is book cover design. The designer will ask for a synopsis of your book and ask about your goals and your intended audience. He or she will then find appropriate images and fonts, and create a design that is in line with similar bestselling books on the market. This ensures that your cover will look as good as, or better than, the competitive titles that will be displayed alongside it online. A good

cover is absolutely essential to the success of your book. Cover design is not the place to save money. Most designers will adjust their services to your budget, if you ask.

Step 2: Manuscript Editing
The benefits of professional editing, offered by an experienced book editor, cannot be overstated. When we read our own writing, we know what we mean to say, so our brain fills in the gaps. The fresh eyes of an outside editor will find and correct these gaps for a smoother reading experience, without changing your style or your voice. Authors can always decline the editor's suggestions, but most are pleasantly surprised at the skills an editor brings to the table.

Step 3: Interior Layout (aka Typesetting)
When editing is complete, the next step in book production is book interior layout, also known as typesetting. Designers usually create one or more sample interior designs to give the author an opportunity to compare different type fonts, type sizes, chapter openers, sidebars, and other decorative elements that may be employed to enhance the appearance of the text. Once a sample chapter has been approved, the rest of the book is typeset to match. You'll be amazed at how much better your text

looks compared to the original Word document, when it is designed by a pro.

Step 4: Proofreading

After interior layout, the next step in the book production process is proofreading. Proofreading should always be done after the book is typeset (and we suggest that it is done before typesetting as well). Those pesky typos, extra word spaces, and unnecessary tabs that escaped detection in Word stand out like a sore thumb in typeset text. Many self-publishers unfortunately decline this service, thinking it's not needed, to the detriment of their book. We have never once proofed a book without finding errors, sometimes hundreds of errors, even when the manuscript had been previously edited.

Step 5: Corrections and Final Review

Once proofreading is complete, and the errors identified by the proofreader (and approved by the author) are fixed, it's time to read the book from start to finish one final time. Even though you just can't stand to read it one more time, you must. There's an old saying in publishing: "You don't complete a book; you declare an ending." The proofreading and correction process never really ends, but at some point you just have to go to press.

Step 6: Digital File Prep
The final step in the production process is to prepare the digital files for printing. You can relax at this stage, because this behind-the-scenes geeky stuff is entirely the responsibility of your designer. This final step ensures that your book will print successfully.

So, How Long Does All This Take?
It's always good to schedule far more time than you think you'll need for book production. We recommend at least two weeks each for steps 1 through 5 above, though some services, such as cover design and editing, can be worked on concurrently. If you must have books in hand by a specific date, be sure to tell your designer, so the two of you, along with the eventual printer, can create a schedule with milestones to make it happen.

How Much of My Time is Required?
That depends on your experience, your personality, and your available time. Many authors relish the "hands-on" approach and enjoy the prospect of talking with multiple providers. Others prefer to hand the project over to a company that will manage the entire project for them. Fortunately, providers are available to suit every preference.

Experts = An Enjoyable Process and a Better Book

The fear of losing control prompts many first-time authors to adopt the "do-it-yourself" approach, or to sign up with huge "self-publishing factories" that produce terrible work for very low fees. Both of these approaches are usually a mistake. Experts abound in every area of life, from medicine to pest control. Their knowledge and experience, even in areas that may seem low-skilled or mundane, enhance our lives and give us far better products and services than we can ever hope to produce on our own. Book design is no exception.

You're about to enter one of the most brutally competitive industries on the planet. We hope this book helps to clarify the book design process so that your experience is an enjoyable one and the book you eventually offer to the public will be the very best it can be—one that you will be proud to market.

Printed Book or eBook? The Parable of the Pumpernickel Baker

Once upon a time, there lived a talented baker named George. Long before dawn each morning, while most people slept, George arrived at his employer's successful bakery. The boss was demanding and grumpy, always

Before You Start

telling George what to bake and when to bake it. "The customer is always right," the boss said.

George would just shake his head and get back to the work he loved—crafting the tastiest varieties of breads, rolls, cakes, cookies, pies, and pot pies that the neighbors had come to expect. Each afternoon, when he left for the day, he said to himself, "Someday, I'll open my own bakery, and I'll bake whatever I want." He saved his money and waited patiently for that day to arrive.

At long last, the perfect building for George's bakery became available. It was located on a busy street, near a bus stop, a school, a factory, and many homes. "This is wonderful," thought George. "I'll have customers all day long and maybe during the factory's night shift, too."

For weeks before the grand opening, everyone in the area eagerly anticipated the breads, rolls, cakes, cookies, pies, and pot pies they'd be able to buy. The factory workers and tired commuters looked forward to a savory, ready-to-eat dinner; the schoolchildren waited for a sweet after-school snack; everyone looked forward to their favorite varieties of breads and rolls.

George was more nervous than he expected, so he played it safe. On Grand Opening Day, customers streamed into George's bakery, but curiously, the only item for sale was pumpernickel bread. Dozens and

dozens of loaves of pumpernickel bread. Nothing else. "Oh, well," they thought, "it's only the first day. Maybe tomorrow there will be more breads, rolls, cakes, cookies, pies, and pot pies." Some customers bought a loaf of pumpernickel bread, because they had waited so long for George's bakery to open, but most customers decided to return the next day.

The next day, and the next, and the next, they gave George another chance, but again they found only pumpernickel bread. Each day, one or two people bought a loaf. Finally, an exasperated customer asked George, "This is a bakery! When will you offer white bread, rolls, cakes, cookies, pies, and pot pies?"

"It's expensive to bake those things," he replied. "I want to make sure my bakery is a success first."

"Oh," said the disappointed customer.

Gradually, the flood of new customers slowed to a trickle. After a few visits, the factory workers went back to brown-bagging it and the schoolchildren realized they would find no cookies at George's bakery. Everyone else reluctantly accepted that George would only offer pumpernickel bread, no matter what they wanted.

Finally, the day came when not one customer showed up. George was puzzled. "Isn't my pumpernickel bread any good?" he wondered. So he walked out front and

Before You Start

stopped a gentleman on the street. "Why don't you come in to my bakery?" he asked.

"Because I don't like pumpernickel bread," the man replied simply. "I buy quite a lot of white bread, cakes, and pies."

"Oh," said George. "But I can't afford to bake those things. At least not until I make some money from my pumpernickel bread."

"Very well," said the gentleman.

We know how this parable ends, don't we? Poor George's bakery failed. He went back to work for his grumpy, demanding boss who understood that it was necessary to give customers what they want.

New publishers who decide to test the market with only an eBook are making exactly the same mistake that George made. They rightly offer their eBook on Amazon and other online retailers where millions of customers can see it 24/7, but then fail to offer the book in other formats that customers want to buy. One new publisher recently told us that she had heard that eBooks are "hot" and an "easy way to make money." Through trial and error she learned that the publisher needs to understand the audience for the book and what medium(s) they prefer.

It's undeniably attractive to publish only an eBook. The costs are minimal and it's scary for any new publisher

 *Publish Like the Pros*

to invest in additional cover design and typesetting for the printed book when the success of the book is uncertain. But guess what? Plenty of people still prefer a printed book, no matter how much eBook devotees bend and twist the statistics. No business owner can lock out a significant portion of their potential market and hope to succeed.

Today, publishers are not just book providers—they are content providers. Consumers want to receive information in different ways at different times. Some people buy printed books to read at home, a welcome change from looking at a computer screen at the office all day. Other people buy eBooks to read at the airport, while yet others listen to audio books while driving. Some consumers buy the same book in multiple formats. It's risky to provide content in only one form. Publishers may sell some books in that format, but it's impossible to count the number of sales that were missed as a result of only offering one format.

Our advice? Offer that eBook, but also do "print on demand" (POD) at Amazon's Kindle Direct Publishing (KDP/www.kdp.com) for Amazon distribution and Ingram Spark (www.ingramspark.com, owned by Lightning Source) for extended distribution. KDP runs its extended distribution through Ingram, but they charge more for the service (60% vs. 55%). Unlike Ingram,

KDP's extended distribution titles are not returnable, so bookstores won't touch them.

While you may balk at the one-time charge for designing the cover and the book interior for the print version when you have already incurred these costs for your eBook, at least you will be offering your book to everyone who may want it, and only printing enough books to fill demand—no stacks of unsold books in your closet. If and when the day arrives that you are selling only eBooks, you can always stop printing.

As Dan Poynter says, "Some writers plan to publish digitally only—to save money. This is a mistake. If you publish an eBook, you are perceived as a writer. If you publish a pBook (paper book), you are regarded as an author. Paper books are retained; files disappear in a click. Self-publishers should offer editions to fit any lifestyle: Paper, eBook, large print for the visually impaired, audio book, etc. Give the buying customer what he or she wants."

Just like George's very smart boss.

CHAPTER TWO

About Your Cover

Book buyers look at a cover for only a few seconds before deciding to buy—or not. In that quick flash of time, a publisher must send a strong subliminal message . . . "This book is good, this book has information you can count on, this book is what you need, this book is going to help you, this book is worth the money."

While it may be tempting to bypass quality book cover and interior design, editing, and proofreading in these challenging economic times, publishers do so at great risk. A book cover that looks ordinary and text that is poorly crafted will not send the right message to your prospective buyer. It will say, instead, "I'm just another book, nothing special; better hold off on spending for now." Would any publisher who hopes to succeed willingly communicate that message?

The same goes for the book's title and back cover copy. While you have invested considerable time and money in writing the book interior, it's really the text on the book cover that counts when it comes to influencing the buyer's decision to purchase your book. The task of writing the book title and back cover copy (text about the book and the author) is quite often left until the end and then rushed. However, if you don't write convincing text for the outside of the book, your readers may never get as far as the inside, so give your title and back cover copy the attention they deserve!

Your Book's Title

The title of your book must make an immediate and positive impression upon the prospective book buyer. It must quickly get to the heart of your book's message; the buyer should understand right away what your book is about, or at least be intrigued enough to pick it up (or scroll down the Amazon page). The book title is, in essence, a promise to the reader and must capture the reader's imagination.

You will need a main title and a subtitle, and your titles must fit well on a book cover (i.e., not too long). If

About Your Cover

your book is part of a series, you need to come up with titles for all the intended books in the series. Make sure the title is not misleading—that it has something to do with the book (while this point might seem obvious, we have seen authors' suggested titles that have nothing to do with their books' subjects!).

It's a good idea to get a book marketing expert to evaluate the strength of your title and to suggest alternatives. Give as much information about the book as possible to the marketing expert. Some of this information is the same as what you would give to a book designer to create cover concepts (see "How Authors Can Help Book Designers" later in this chapter). For example, you need to let the book marketing expert know your intended audience and market, and if possible, provide a manuscript or at least a synopsis of the book. Based on this information, he or she will create alternative titles that drill right down to a message that the book's buyer will understand.

Back Cover Copy

Imagine a book buyer reading the text on the back cover of your book. What information do you think he or she is looking for? When you get down to it, the only thing the prospective buyer is interested in is, "What's in it for me?" The book buyer wants to know what he or she will get out of reading your book. Why should they invest time and money in reading your book? If the answer to these questions is not found on the back cover, chances are you will lose a potential customer.

Remember that the cover text—back and front—may be your only opportunity to communicate with a prospective reader. It's your sales pitch! Unfortunately, many authors blow this opportunity to tell the reader all about the book, and instead write back cover text that details the background of the book, why he or she wrote it, and why the book is meaningful—to the author. Here are some hints for writing great back cover copy:

- Know your audience and your market and speak directly to them.

- Get inside your reader's head. Pretend that you are explaining the book to your ideal reader. After listening to you, what would your reader say are the benefits of reading your book?

- The text should compel readers to take action, and the action you want them to take is to buy the book.

About Your Cover

- If your book is fiction, provide a brief synopsis of the plot, but don't give away the entire book. Your readers don't want to learn what happens in your book by reading it on the back cover.

- The author biography should appear on the back cover. It should be very brief and focused on your expert credentials; readers want to know your background and why you are qualified to write this book, particularly if your book is nonfiction. We recommend that you don't include your photo here, so that the bulk of the space on the back cover can be used for the sales pitch. A longer author bio and picture can be used inside the book.

- Keep the text short, simple and focused. For a nonfiction book, use bullet points for the benefits—what the reader will get out of the book. The average book buyer will spend no more than ten seconds reading your back cover text, so make sure that you can get your message across quickly.

- Hire a book marketing expert to ensure that you will make an immediate and positive impact in a short amount of time, and to give your book the best possible chance to sell.

Cover Design

Your designer should provide you with a selection of cover concepts, each of which should be very different from one another to give you a clear choice of direction. The purpose of cover research is to identify and develop three major design directions that are represented in current bestsellers for your genre. A cover concept is not one image shown with three different title fonts. Those are variations. It's important to ask your designer whether they plan to show you concepts or variations.

Naturally, concepts take more time than variations. Time is money in every line of work. Allowing your designer to spend the necessary time to develop truly creative solutions will benefit your book many times over. Why? Because humans are programmed from birth to look longer at things we haven't seen before. In prehistoric times, this instinct saved us from the saber-toothed tiger prowling outside the cave. Today, it means your buyer will look longer at your cover if it's interesting and different, and the longer buyers look, the more likely they are to buy.

If you look closely at low-cost covers, you'll see they are really template-driven; they are all the same. Designers who produce this type of cover are taking care of themselves, not you. They're telling you what you want to hear—that you can get a cover for a few hundred dollars—but they're not giving you what you need to succeed. Boring covers are just that, boring. Buyers will gravitate to and buy books with covers that are visually compelling.

How Authors Can Help Book Designers

There's quite a bit of misinformation floating around about book designers and the book design process. Some folks think designers are creative psychics who somehow just know what to do, without any help from the client. Nothing is further from the truth. There are thousands of ways to design a book cover. A competent book cover designer will start by gathering information that will help him or her design your cover in an appropriate way. Here's how you, the author or publisher, can help before design begins:

- Provide a manuscript, or at least a synopsis, of your book (a draft version is okay).

- Provide the final title and subtitle of the book and the author's name as you wish it to appear on the cover (including any professional designations).

- Provide any logos that are to appear on the front cover.

- Decide on the book's trim size and the number of print colors. If you're not sure about these issues, your designer can help.

- Share your vision for the cover.

- Share information about your intended audience/market.

- Tell the designer whether this book is part of a series. Series covers need to be developed with future titles in mind.

- Share any other information you feel will help the designer understand your book. There's no such thing as too much information.

Once the above items are known, your designer will research other books in the genre and create several concepts of the front cover for your review.

Getting an ISBN

Because your ISBN will be printed on your book cover in the form of a bar code, this is a good time to talk about how to get one. ISBN is the acronym for "International Standard Book Number," which is the global identification number for books. ISBNs are available in the US from

About Your Cover

Bowker (www.myidentifiers.com). Because you need a separate ISBN for each version of your book (hardcover, softcover, various electronic formats), we recommend that you save money by purchasing a block of ten ISBNs.

It's a good idea to include the bar code on your back cover if you plan on selling your book through a retail outlet. The bar code allows for automated scanning and point-of-sale transactions. We recommend that you get one no matter what; it's professional and you will have more flexibility in terms of where you decide to sell your book. Even if you don't intend on selling your book at a bookstore, book fair or other retail outlet right now, with an ISBN and a bar code on your cover, you have the option of changing your mind in the future. Bar codes will be offered at www.myidentifiers.com when you purchase your ISBNs, but don't rush to buy them. Most book cover designers include bar codes for free.

If you are confused about ISBNs and bar codes, talk to your book designer, who should be familiar with the purchase of both. Beware of some self-publishing companies or POD publishers who may pressure you to use one of their ISBNs. By using an ISBN that is part of a block already assigned to another company, you are telling the world that the other company is the publisher and not you.

CHAPTER THREE

Editing

After a thorough edit by a professional, your book will stand up to the tough scrutiny of distributors, reviewers, retailers, and libraries. There are three types of editing: copyediting, substantive editing and proofreading. The lines between each editing service can be blurry and hence, confusing for a self-publisher to determine exactly what is needed.

Copyediting entails a comprehensive edit of your book. The editor will look at spelling, grammar, punctuation, word choice, paragraph structure, flow and style consistency. Most copyeditors will also catch outright errors in your manuscript. As we say, a second set of eyes is invaluable!

With a substantive edit, the editor goes beyond a copyedit and checks the structure of your book, often moving parts of the text around to correct the logical flow of the material. Material that is redundant or does not fit is flagged for your attention, and areas where more writing is required are highlighted. Substantive edits are excellent for authors who are unsure of their writing skills or who sense a problem with their manuscript that they just can't put their finger on.

For the purposes of clarification, we included proofreading as an editing function; however, it should not be confused with copyediting. Proofreading is a necessary step in the book production process. A proofreader will check for typos and punctuation but will not agonize over your choice of words or sentence structure, or figure out the problem with your manuscript, fix it and piece the book back together again. A copyedit or substantive edit goes well beyond catching typos, adding that extra level of professionalism and readability that make your book stand out from the others. However, proofreading is very important, and because it should be done in addition to editing, we have given this important step its own chapter later in this book.

The Importance of Editing

It's a major achievement to write a book. The typical author spends an inordinate amount of time on a manuscript—going over it, perfecting it, taking this bit out or adding that bit in, and then taking it out again. Subsequently, the author becomes too close to the material to be objective; after many rewrites and even more readings, the author's brain "fills in the blanks" and sees what it expects to see. You may know what you mean to say, but the text may be less clear to someone reading it for the first time. Remember, your readers will read your book in a much different manner than you! The fresh eyes of an editor can be a real benefit (and we don't mean just for proofreading).

If you decide to let someone else look at your book for the purposes of a final thorough copyedit, beware of giving it to a friend or relative who happens to be an English teacher. Hiring an experienced editor is very important; your relatives are not trained to have an editor's eye or an editor's sense of logic and flow. A good editor does much more than fix your grammar; he or she improves a book's content and structure in a way that preserves the author's style. A good editor will place him- or herself in the shoes of your readers and determine where a reader might find your book confusing, repetitive, redundant or shallow. Just as important, he or she finds and corrects both major and minor errors.

For example, our editor once found a mistake in a cookbook—a collection of easy supper recipes using precooked rotisserie chickens from the grocery store. At the front of the book, the author provided a warning that these recipes were to be made only with cooked chicken, never with uncooked chicken. All well and good. But our editor noticed that within each recipe itself, the list of ingredients simply said "chicken." Of course, the author knew what she meant, but in real life, people flip through a cookbook and don't always re-read the first pages. This one little correction, changing "chicken" to "cooked chicken," probably prevented a lot of bellyaches (or worse).

Having your book edited is money well spent. An editor won't rob you of your style; instead, he or she will enhance it. Many freelance editors have their own websites, in which they outline their credentials, philosophy of editing, and rates. Try and select an editor who is experienced in fiction or nonfiction, depending on the nature of your book, particularly for a substantive edit. For example, an editor whose expertise is in children's books is probably not the best person to edit your economics

Editing

textbook. Once you've contacted an editor about possibly working with him or her, the editor will generally ask to see a sample of your book. Have no fear that the editor is going to steal your book idea; the purpose of looking at your book is to give you an accurate price quote, so there is no misunderstanding later.

CHAPTER FOUR
Interior Layout

Your book design, inside and out, establishes your credibility in the eyes of the buyer. Buyers may not be able to pinpoint exactly what is wrong with the pages of your book, but without a professional interior design, your book will not measure up to those that are professionally prepared. For the success of your new publishing endeavor, we hope you'll give this issue some serious thought and choose an experienced book designer to give your book the professional look it deserves.

Why Your Book Layout Needs a Professional Touch

We have heard this question many times: "Should I lay out the interior of my book

Publish Like the Pros

myself?" Seems like a no-brainer. You have word processing software. You know how to set margins and choose a typeface. You even know of books that describe the process (written by folks who are not trained in typography, by the way). So why shouldn't you lay out your own book?

Of course you can and should use your word processing software to write your text, but interior design and formatting are best left to people who do this for a living. There are many elements involved in a successful interior design. Size, binding, paper, page layout and typography work together to present your subject matter in an appropriate and attractive way. An experienced book designer creates appealing pages that hold interest and convince the reader that your book is the one to buy. If the interior design of your book doesn't surprise and delight you, don't expect it to impress anyone else.

Word processing software does not have the sophisticated hyphenation and justification controls that professional page layout software does, resulting in tight and loose lines that are unsightly and that distract the reader. Page layout software has a very steep learning curve; these products are complicated and assume a good knowledge of typography. As the saying goes, "Owning a hammer does not make one a carpenter." Renting software "in the cloud" requires an active subscription to alter your book files in the future, so this option is not as inexpensive as it seems at first glance.

Quality typesetting has never been about the tools. In fact, it's a mistake to assume that no knowledge of typography or design is required to use the software effectively. Don't assume that you can make up for lack of knowledge by using the software's default settings. Experienced typesetters rarely use software at the default settings. We adjust the settings for better results, sometimes paragraph by paragraph, line by line, and even word by word. Why? We were trained to see the difference between "so-so" type and great type. As such, there are several dozen conventions to be followed in book design that may not be perceptible to the reader, but when followed, they give your book a polished appearance. But it's not only about knowing the rules; it's knowing how and when to bend or break them on a case-by-case basis that makes the difference between an amateur layout and a professional one.

For what it's worth, only beginner self-publishers consider using a word processor for page layout. Established publishers wouldn't think of producing the text in this manner. They know that experienced book designers bring real value to the table, offering creativity and aesthetic judgment that only comes with training and experience.

Here's a before-and-after example. *Seven Principles for Happiness* (Before) (https://bit.ly/2YqJ4Yi) is the client's attempt at designing the title page. *Seven Principles for Happiness* (After) (https://bit.ly/3t8R3qK) is our design (The title changed along the way). (You may want to open or print both images to compare the pages side-by-side.) See the difference? The "before" example looks something like a book, and the author, who eventually became our client, thought it was just fine . . . until he saw our "after" version. This wasn't an isolated occurrence. When we show customers the difference between their attempt at book layout and our own every day, they are usually blown away. They'll say something like, "Wow! I thought my layout was just fine. Now I see how bad it really is!"

Here's another example. Compare this page from *Fat Loss* (Before) (https://bit.ly/3ps9yo8) with *Fat Loss* (After) (https://bit.ly/3cofxXc), which shows how a designer can improve the look and functionality of a table in addition to making the page more appealing. Not only does the "after" version look better, but the overall design improvements that we made saved pages and reduced the author's printing costs substantially. So, design isn't just about decoration (as Steve Jobs once said); it's about printing efficiency too!

Interior Layout

Many people think that all a printer needs is a word-processed file that has been converted to a PDF. This is what the POD publishers tell people, and they are right; but it's not all that YOU need. Printers won't turn away a PDF that was made from a word-processed document. They don't care how it got to be a PDF or how the book was designed in the first place, and most printers are too polite to tell you the truth about how your book looks. They'll print your book because that's what they're in business to do. Their success is measured in how many books they print. Your success, on the other hand, is measured in the number of books you sell. And an amateur job won't satisfy the distributors, reviewers and book retailers—the "gatekeepers" of the book industry—who will immediately spot a beginner's efforts and reject your book as "self-published." As a side note, quality typography improves reading comprehension—it has been clinically proven!

Novels, directories, reference books, computer manuals and magazines each require a different approach to page layout. Successful page layout invites the reader in and subtly leads the eye from one section to the next. The right fonts, careful spacing, and a pleasing arrangement work together to make reading a pleasure instead of a chore. An experienced typesetter has the tools to carefully

Publish Like the Pros

adjust justification, word spacing, and letter spacing to give your text an even "color" that's easy on the eyes, and, as a bonus, delivers better reading comprehension.

Another way to make your book stand out is to adopt an unusual page size and orientation. Standard sizes exist primarily for printing efficiency, but that doesn't obligate you to use them. "Standard" is another way to say "ordinary." With a few limitations imposed by bindery equipment, a book can be almost any size or shape—horizontal, vertical, square, oval or even a star.

Paper can also enhance your book. You don't have to use white. There are hundreds of papers in a variety of colors, weights and finishes. Your designer can show you samples and help you choose a paper that enhances your message, feels good in the hand, and adds a sense of value to your book.

While "nonstandard" options will cost more, they could provide the visual interest that causes the buyer to stop and look at your book.

When all the elements of good design work in harmony, the result is a beautiful book, inside and out. Your manuscript represents an enormous effort. Creative interior design will bring it to life—make it a "real" book that you can promote with pride and more importantly, sell.

Interior Layout

What Do Book Designers Really Do?

With word processing tools now available to everyone, book design has become a misunderstood craft. It's not uncommon for book designers to receive a request to "convert my Word file into a PDF for the printer." Like the book printers who will print your book without telling you the truth about how it looks, there are some so-called designers who will go ahead and convert your file, no questions asked. The result will be . . . um . . . just like your Word file and nothing like a real book. So what does a professional book designer really do?

The first thing a book designer will do is create a sample chapter. There are multiple ways to design any book, and for this reason a book designer will normally develop several samples. These samples will include subtleties in the use of font styles and sizes that make a book look like a real book, and not a word-processed document. We always choose fonts and images that are in keeping with your subject matter to give your book a unique (and appropriate) look. Once these initial concepts are presented, it's necessary to work back and forth with the author/publisher until all the details are hammered out. Only then is the rest of the book typeset to match the sample.

Note that while it's normal to expect a book designer to provide you with sample designs for your project as a first step AFTER hiring the designer, it's bad form to expect these samples for free as a basis for your hiring decision. Book designers are trained professionals and should not be expected to work for free. However, it's perfectly acceptable to ask for samples of previous work and for client testimonials before making your decision.

Here are just a few of the things book designers will do during the layout process:

- Ensure facing pages end on the same baseline without the first line of a paragraph landing on the bottom of a page, or the last line of a paragraph landing on the top of a page. When the text doesn't cooperate with these rules (which is often), the book designer will rework previous paragraphs and pages as needed.

- Fix paragraphs where the last line consists only of a word with less than five characters (including punctuation) or a word fragment (the stub end of a hyphenated word).

- Banish "ladders" (too many hyphens in a row) and find and fix hyphenated compound words, both of which distract the reader.

Interior Layout

- Eliminate word stacks—when the same word falls one above the other on several consecutive lines of text.

- Adjust any overly tight or loose lines that software sometimes allows to slip through.

- Watch for and eliminate "rivers" of white in the text—when word spaces fall in a pattern that is distracting to the reader.

- Eliminate hyphens at the bottom of a right-hand page so that the reader won't have to hold a thought while the page is turned.

- Make sure the last page of a chapter has at least four lines of text.

(The above bullets are adapted from the book "Digital Type Design Guide" by Sean Cavanaugh. © 1995 Hayden Books, a division of Macmillan Computer Publishing.)

We fix all these issues and more. Software out of the box only goes so far . . . it is this level of human intervention that turns your manuscript into typographic art and a professional masterpiece, and when you see the results, we know you'll agree that this time is well spent.

Publish Like the Pros

Get the Most from Your Book Design Dollar

The mantra "Plan Now or Pay Later" is true in just about every area of life, but especially so in book design. Professional design and typesetting help your book stand out and sell better. Book designers and typesetters want you to get the most for your money. But you have an important role to play in delivering a top-notch product on time and at a reasonable price.

Here is the most important thing you can do to control costs: once your manuscript is complete—STOP. What do we mean by "complete"? Inevitably you want people in your circle to read your book—your friends, relatives, trusted colleagues and others. Make sure that everyone who you want to read the book has done so, and that you have implemented any changes that resulted from their reviews. When you are satisfied with the results, hire a professional editor to read the manuscript. Once you have implemented the editor's changes, don't be tempted to send it out to your circle of friends again! This is the time to STOP. A book should be edited only once, with the possible addition of a targeted edit on any areas your editor might have felt were problematic and needed reworking.

The editing and typesetting process is turned on its head when major textual changes are made after the editing is supposedly complete. Why? If you ask an editor to go well beyond what they were hired to do, say, by asking them to do a second, third or fourth complete copyedit on your manuscript, they are justified in requesting additional funds. And typesetting a book is not at all like revising a manuscript. Once page layout begins, seemingly minor changes can quickly add up. Adding a sentence to your manuscript in a word processor takes a few seconds and costs nothing. Adding that same sentence after your book is laid out may cause all the text after it to reflow, and require time-consuming layout adjustments. All this is to say that making changes after you should have stopped can add up to big bucks!

Another way to control book design costs is to pay close attention to the sample chapters that your designer will offer, and work together until you're satisfied with the type style, type size and layout. Changing this sample is usually free; making changes to the design after hundreds of pages have already been formatted can quickly become expensive.

And here's another important money-saving tip: Understand the difference between changes and corrections, both of which are inevitable during the typesetting process. These may sound alike, but they're not. A change, or author's alteration (AA), is exactly that. A misspelled name is considered a chargeable AA, because only the author can reasonably be expected to know the information. The number of chargeable AAs can be reduced by proofreading your manuscript before typesetting. More about proofreading in the next chapter.

A correction, or typesetter error (TE), should always be fixed free of charge. Typesetting a subhead in the wrong font is an example of a nonchargeable TE. Marking your proofs with these abbreviations will give everyone a sense of how the job is going and avoid hard feelings at billing time.

If, despite your best efforts, you must make changes to your page proofs, you can still save money by doing it efficiently.

First, make all your changes in one pass. It takes many hours to change an entire book multiple times. Consolidate your changes into one or two rounds and you won't have to deal with "sticker shock" later.

Second, add several weeks to your prepress schedule for changes. It's stressful for everyone and unfair to your typesetter to hold to the original deadline when days or weeks of work have been added to the project. If you finish early, you can celebrate.

One final tip: If you make changes, expect to pay for them. Everyone wants the job to go smoothly. Your

Interior Layout

typesetter's written estimate should specify how many hours of revisions are included, and quote an hourly rate for changes beyond that. If you don't see these items, be sure to ask. If you do see them, talk it over. If the written estimate includes words such as "reasonable revisions," clarify upfront what the typesetter considers to be "reasonable." Know however, that if you return a typeset manuscript chock-full of mark-ups and revisions, you can expect additional charges over and above what is included in your estimate for "reasonable revisions." If you DO have extensive revisions to a typeset manuscript, your typesetter should be able to give you an estimate of how long these additional changes will take and what they will cost you.

    A little planning can help everyone involved to produce your book on time and on budget, with publisher and designer alike looking forward to the next one.

CHAPTER FIVE

Proofreading

SOME AUTHORS THINK they don't need proofreading after layout, because their manuscript was edited, or because they proofread it themselves in Word before typesetting. (Beware! Word does not spellcheck in context!) We just shake our heads and sigh, because an experienced book proofreader will typically find hundreds, and sometimes thousands, of errors.

Why You Should Proofread Your Book Before Typesetting

Consider having your book proofed by a professional before sending it for typesetting. If, in the process of implementing the editor's changes and suggestions, you have written new text or shifted around parts of your book, you may have created new typos and other errors over and above those caught by the editor. Discuss the need to proofread your manuscript with your editor. Consider how carefully you inputted any changes. Remember that any changes made after typesetting may be more costly than those done before because it's more time consuming (and therefore, more expensive) to make changes to the file after the layout is complete.

In the end, it's up to you, because you are the one footing the bill. But the few hundred dollars that it might cost to have your book professionally proofread before typesetting may be a worthwhile expense.

Why You Should Proofread Your Book After Typesetting

One of our team members recently read a book by a well-known book coach. The author's advice was rock solid and our team member enjoyed the book immensely, but she reported that something had gone terribly wrong during the book's production. There were errors on nearly every page! The errors were so numerous that we're guessing the wrong version of the manuscript was accidentally typeset, and because the pages were not proofread after typesetting, the errors were not discovered before printing.

Proofreading

Back in "the day," book publishing followed a standard procedure: The manuscript was edited and proofread multiple times. Only when all the editors, the author, and senior staff signed off on the manuscript did it go into production (typesetting).

Before desktop publishing, typeset "galleys" were produced, meaning, the type was set in long strips of paper, produced by the phototypesetting machines of the era. These galleys were sent to the author, and reviewed yet again by editors and staff. Corrections were made, and only then was the book "pasted up" into pages and sent to the printer.

While the procedure sounds archaic now, it did accomplish one major goal: Corrections were very rare after the book was paginated. Today, with desktop publishing equipment, pages are made and changed, sometimes multiple times. And sometimes, NOBODY reads the pages after they have been typeset—a dangerous practice indeed.

Regardless of whether the book is proofed before typesetting, it is essential that it be proofed after typesetting; something about seeing your book when it looks like a REAL book seems to make typos and errors jump from the page, even pages that have been edited and proofed previously. Most typesetters will call your attention to typos or text that sound odd, if they happen to notice an error while formatting; however don't depend on typesetters to proof your book. They are not experts in your field and should not change your content or punctuation. Imagine the havoc that would ensue if they did! So again, hire a professional proofreader to do this final proof of your book.

In the meantime, please understand that when your book designer encourages you to order professional proofreading after your pages are typeset, there's a really, really, good reason.

CHAPTER SIX

Book Distribution, Pricing and Marketing

TO REPEAT WHAT WAS SAID at the beginning of this book, it's essential that you treat your self-publishing project as a business. You have a product to sell: your book. You've invested hundreds of hours of time in developing your product and hundreds—if not thousands—of dollars in creating and polishing it, turning it into a product that you know consumers will buy. But you would be surprised how many authors fail to think past this point and end up allowing the self-publishing company to "distribute" the book (with average sales of fifty books) or who have a stack of book cartons in their garage, unsold. So, it's important to think about how you are going to market your book to your potential readers, what price you are going to charge, and then, how you are going to get it to them!

Book Distribution

Why do authors self-publish their books? To make sure they get put into print! Self-publishing has allowed authors to bypass publishers—the traditional gatekeepers for determining what gets printed and what doesn't. In the good old days, only publishers had access to book distribution, the conduits available for getting a book to the customer—the end reader. Thus, in order to distribute a book, an author needed to have it accepted by a publisher. Amazon and other online retailers have changed all that. Now authors can also become the distributor by listing their books directly on a website.

Since self-publishing takes the traditional publisher out of the picture, the onus is now on the author to figure out how to get the book into readers' hands. This is the distribution function, and it's one in which the author, as publisher, must take an active role. While you could also think of distribution as selling your book, please don't confuse it with marketing, which is addressed in the next section. Marketing is the act of informing people about your book. If people don't know about your book, no amount of distribution will get them to buy it! And even if you work with a distributor, some do not market your book beyond listing it in a database or catalog; they will assume that you are fulfilling the marketing function. This is why a POD publisher's promise to make your book available to all bookstores nationwide rings hollow. Putting your book on a database is passive; you have to choose how active you are going to be in marketing your book.

So, as a self-publisher, what are your options for distributing your book? Here are a few ideas. Note that there are pluses and minuses for each option (time involved, expense, amount of money that goes to the online retailer, and so on), so investigate them thoroughly before making a commitment.

- Have a table at a book fair. Many towns have book fairs that welcome authors to sell their books.

- Approach your library and ask them how they purchase books. You should know however, that small libraries tend to have small budgets for book purchases and they share books through library networks. Consider donating a book to the library so that it is available on the network to share. By doing so, you may raise awareness about your

book—and possible demand—so that copies of your book are purchased.

- Be an exhibitor at a conference that relates to the topic of your book. Tables can be quite cheap, and can often be shared, at local or regional conferences; you don't need a full-blown exhibit.

- Better yet, be a speaker at a conference and ask to sell your books at the back of the room.

- Think of other venues that may welcome you to sell your book at one of their fairs, or in their lobby during lunchtime, especially if you offer to donate a percentage of your sales (e.g., your faith community, community center, retirement home, Humane Society, hospital).

- Approach independent bookstores and gift shops to take your book. Some will take your book on consignment so that they don't have to invest money in inventory of an unproven product.

- Create your own website and sell your book there via PayPal or other shopping cart software. You will fulfill and ship the orders, so make sure you have stock on hand, along with mailing supplies!

Book Distribution, Pricing and Marketing

- Sell your book through Amazon. There are a number of ways to do so; please check their website (www.amazon.com) for up-to-date details of their various seller programs. Note that you are not required to self-publish through their company KDP in order to place your book on Amazon.

- If you print on demand via Ingram Spark (www.ingramspark.com), write to one of their representatives about distribution and how your book can be distributed through their partners. Ingram Spark automatically feeds titles to Amazon and other online retailers, sending payments directly to the author. This is the easiest way to get your book in front of the most readers without spending thousands of dollars up front for offset printing. But remember! They won't do any marketing.

- Purchase Dan Poynter's books on successful self-publishing. He has a few titles:
Behind the Self-Publishing Boom, Print-on-Demand and E-Book Publishing (for more information, see www.u-publish.com); *The Self-Publishing Manual: How to Write, Print and Sell Your Own Book* (Volumes 1 and 2). Because the industry is

Publish Like the Pros

changing so rapidly, be sure that you purchase the most recent versions of his books.

▸ Contact a marketing and distribution specialist. New Shelves Distribution (www.newshelves.com) and Brian Jud (www.bookmarketingworks.com) offer book marketing and distribution packages to fit almost every budget, and are available for free consultations to determine your requirements.

How to Determine Your Book's Price

What should you charge customers for your book? There are two prices that you need to calculate: the retail price and the wholesale price.

For the purposes of this discussion, we are going to assume that you are using Ingram Spark (www.ingramspark.com) to print your book on demand and to distribute it to their distribution partners: Ingram Book, Amazon, Baker & Taylor, Barnes & Noble and others. Ingram Spark's distribution partners pay the wholesale price for each book.

The end retail outlets will charge the retail price to the end buyer. This is the price that will be printed on your book cover and encoded in the bar code. This price is only a suggested retail price; retailers have already paid for the book and if they decide to charge less to the end

Book Distribution, Pricing and Marketing

customer, the price difference will come out of their margin (the difference between what they paid for the book and what they charge the customer). Thus, when Amazon marks down a book, they are reducing their revenue from the book because they have already paid for it.

The wholesale price will be approximately 45 percent of your retail price. For example, if the retail price for your book is $10.00, the wholesale price will be $4.50. This is the price that wholesalers such as Amazon will pay to you. You will frequently see the term "wholesale discount." While your book might be priced at $10.00, the wholesalers are being given a 55 percent discount by being able to purchase your book at $4.50 ($10 × 1-wholesaler discount of 55 percent = $4.50).

Out of the $4.50 that you receive from wholesalers, you must pay for printing. Ingram Spark will provide you with a per book printing cost. Let's say that in this case your book costs $2.50 to print. $4.50 − $2.50 means that your revenue from each book is $2.00. For this you are getting orders fulfilled on demand and you are receiving regular checks from Ingram Spark for any purchases made by their wholesale partners.

When you look at the difference between the retail price ($10) and the wholesale price ($4.50), you may be tempted to dispense with "wholesale partners" altogether and sell your book by yourself via your own website, at book fairs, or at a table at conferences. While companies such as Amazon take their "pound of flesh" as some authors like to say, an author cannot match the reach of an online retailer. By all means you can and should create your own website to promote and sell your book, but your website should not be the only source for buyers. Would you rather sell 20 books at a profit of $7.50 ($10 − $2.50 printing costs) for a total of $150.00, or 200 books at a profit of $2 for a total of $400?

Selling the book by yourself without Amazon or other distribution outlets has its own set of costs. For example, if you use PayPal on your website to accept payments, a fee is deducted for each sale. If you sell at a book fair, you will pay a fee for the table. If you sell your books at a conference, there are shipping costs to get your books to the venue. And you will have to make an upfront investment in book printing to ensure you have stock on hand for selling; using the Amazon scenario, you only pay printing for the books you sell. In addition, even though you might sell your book on your website, many potential customers will visit your site, then look for it on Amazon, and if they can't find it there, they won't buy it at all.

Here are some other considerations to take into account when determining your retail book price:

Book Distribution, Pricing and Marketing

- The price of other books in your genre. Don't price yourself out of the market.

- Do not include one-time costs such as book design, editing, typesetting and proofreading or consulting fees. You should be aware of these costs when creating your budget so that you know how much money is available to invest in these vital services.

- Your profit will determine how much you can comfortably spend marketing your book.

- If you sell your book on consignment to retail outlets that are willing to consider this arrangement, the "wholesale discount" should be less than 55 percent, meaning that your profit will be higher.

- Supplement your book revenues by using some of the suggested distribution methods listed in the previous section.

- Amazon has various seller programs, each with their associated benefits, drawbacks and costs to you. You should investigate all the options before committing.

- Marketing experts suggest different approaches to pricing books. Some will say that the retail price

is a product of the printing cost (for example, Dan Poynter says that the retail price should be eight times the printing cost). Others will suggest looking at the range of prices for similar books in the same genre as a starting point. Even if you use the printing cost methodology, you should make sure that the end retail cost is within the range of comparable books.

▶ Book buyers who purchase directly from you will want to know if there is a volume discount for purchases of multiple books, especially if your book is one that could be used for a class or a group.

A Marketing Plan for Your Book

The following list presents components of a possible marketing plan for your book. Consider what is feasible for you given your time and budget. Some of these points might seem a little repetitive of the ideas for distributing your book. Well, there is some overlap, to be sure. For example, we suggested in the section on distribution that you ask a bookstore to take your book on consignment. But remember; you have to let them know about your book first. So, the following list of marketing ideas suggests that you prepare a mailing to bookstores, gift shops and other stores. First you need to know where you are selling your book, then you need to figure out how to a) convince people to let you sell it there, and b) convince readers to buy it. That's marketing.

Website Promotions

- Create a website. The domain name should reflect the name of the book. The content on the site should include keywords that you think your audience may search for when investigating the subject matter of your book.

- Register the website with the top ten search engines. The "top ten" is an ever-changing list, so when your website is complete, Google "register for top 10 search engines" and you should find an article listing the top 10 with links to their "submit url" page.

- Have sample pages available for people to review. These can be added to your website.

- Approach people (family, friends, colleagues, respected people in your field or the field addressed by your book) to read a proof copy specifically to get their testimonials and feedback. You can contact people via e-mail, telephone or regular mail to make the request. These testimonials can then be used on your website, on your Amazon page, on your book cover, sell sheets, bookmarks and postcards—anywhere that a testimonial will help convince a buyer to purchase your book. Prospective book buyers take these reviews seriously, and you will find that eventually people you don't know will start leaving reviews on your Amazon page, website or Facebook page!

- Use the "Look Inside!" feature on Amazon. Many buyers take the opportunity to "look inside" to review the table of contents, index, preface and random sample pages before making their purchasing decision.

- Offer a free monthly electronic newsletter to anyone who visits the site. Newsletter content can include samples from the book, inspirational messages, and a reminder that the book is still available for purchase.

- Create and sell merchandise with the name of the book (coffee cups, mouse pads, Frisbee, etc.). Make sure you have permission to use any images that you print on merchandise. For example, you may only have permission to use your book cover

Book Distribution, Pricing and Marketing

image on promotional items that you give away and not those that you sell.

- Find opportunities for reciprocal promotion. For example, swap display ads with other websites featuring books, writers, authors, etc.

- Investigate online affiliate programs, where a percentage of your sales go to an individual or organization in return for promoting your book to their audience.

- Participate in online author chats.

- Include a "press room" on your site where media reps can visit and see relevant information, including a book review, author bio, FAQs, etc. Have an online press kit available for download on your website.

- Include a blog on your website. Update your blog with new content at least once a week (daily updates are not required and are in fact, overkill). Promote any updates via social media.

- Utilize social networking websites, including Facebook, Twitter, LinkedIn and others to promote the book. Include plug-ins on your website for the

Publish Like the Pros

various social media sites, so that users only need to click on that button to "like" your Facebook page or follow you on Twitter.

Media Promotions

- Send press releases to local and regional media outlets, and to newspapers featuring book reviews.

- Create an "author interview" blurb and send to programming directors at radio stations that feature author interviews. Radio and TV producers are especially receptive to such contacts when news on your subject is breaking.

- Create a professional video "book trailer" and put it on YouTube.com. Promote it through your social media sites and hope it goes "viral"!

- Send press releases to relevant print, broadcast and online outlets that feature articles about books and author interviews.

Library Promotions

- Send press releases to local and regional libraries.

- Visit local and regional libraries; offer to hold a presentation about the book.

Book Distribution, Pricing and Marketing

Personal Appearances

- Contact bookstores within a fifty-mile radius and offer to do a book signing and presentation.

- Contact colleges and universities and offer to host a one-hour lecture about the book.

- Contact local schools and offer to do an author visit to classrooms.

- Offer to teach at local, regional and national conferences.

- Contact relevant associations and offer to speak at their next event; offer excerpts from your book for their newsletters and website.

Miscellaneous Promotions

- Mail a postcard, with the book cover art on one side, to family members, friends, business associates, etc. The other side will be a request for them to share the info with at least five friends, and information on how to order the book. Your book designer can design a postcard and other giveaways, such as bookmarks.

- Create a "sell sheet" and e-mail it to the top fifty independent bookstores. Here again, the homemade sell sheet isn't going to look the same as one designed by a pro.

- Mail a postcard or sell sheet to local stores and gift shops (other than bookstores) and ask them to carry the book. Follow up with a personal call; offer to provide them on consignment. Be available for a book signing, author presentation, etc.

- Offer copies of the book as prizes for various contests, door prizes at conferences, or gifts for conference speakers.

- Contact the local Chamber of Commerce, Lion's Club and other service organizations and offer to be a guest speaker at an upcoming event. Be sure to ask to sell books after the event. Investigate speaking at their regional or national conferences.

- Offer to make an appearance at local and regional book fairs and festivals.

- Participate in a teleseminar or webinar, which are used to provide information, to train a group of people or to promote a product. Teleseminars and webinars give you the opportunity to be interviewed by another expert and present yourself as a resource.

Conclusion

Now that you have finished reading this book, we hope you are feeling more comfortable, confident and better informed about self-publishing. You have your "publisher" hat firmly on your head and are already dreaming about your publisher imprint. (Oh, did we mention that you should have an imprint, or logo? That's okay. Most book designers can help you with that too!)

As a publisher, you have identified the players in the field. You discern between self-publishing companies and POD printers, and you know that you can hire all the services necessary to produce your book professionally. You may be feeling a little uncomfortable about how much these services are going to cost, but after reading this book, you've realized some pretty important things. First, the process of producing your book must be treated as a business, complete with a budget, and a marketing and distribution plan. Second, your book is your product, and your product must be of the utmost quality, one that people are going to want to purchase—or what's the point? And third, to produce a book that stands out from all the other books—one that doesn't scream "self-published" and instead is a book that intrigues potential readers and makes them want to buy it—you may just need to bring in some experts. By carefully identifying your needs, evaluating your options, taking advantage of free consultations offered by experts, and avoiding the package "deals" available through POD publishers, you can assess the services you need, and hire the professional(s) you require to make your book the best it can be without breaking the bank.

If you're still not sure and you need a little help in publishing business finance and management, we recommend contacting Marion Gropen, a financial and management consultant to publishers. Advice is delivered question by question or in do-it-yourself packages. See www.GropenAssoc.com.

Now down to actual book production. After assessing your needs and available options, you've made the decision NOT to lay out your book using Word, NOT to purchase that expensive page layout software package, and NOT to use the handy-dandy downloadable templates from the POD publisher website. You want book buyers to take your

Conclusion

book seriously, so you want the cover and interior to look as professional and polished as possible. You've started to identify book designers, perhaps through referrals from other self-publishers or perhaps by doing some research on the web. You're almost ready to make the call for a free consultation with a book designer. After you've chosen your book designer, you're excited about seeing some cover concepts and interior page design samples.

Even though your Aunt Tilly, the schoolteacher, has read your manuscript and given it her stamp of approval, you've decided to go ahead and hire an editor. You're feeling pretty good about the quality of your manuscript, so you're going with a thorough copyedit rather than a substantive edit. Then, after you've made changes to the manuscript, you're going to hire a proofreader to catch typos and other errors before the book goes for typesetting. No sense paying extra money to have the typesetter fix all the errors after the book is already laid out! But you know that a proofreader will need to give the book another once-over after the book is formatted to catch the pesky errors that almost got away.

You've taken the parable of the pumpernickel baker to heart, and have decided to produce both a printed book and an eBook. You took a look at the Ingram Spark website and have decided to go with print-on-demand (or traditional offset printing, if your business model requires it). You also went to the Bowker website and are looking forward to purchasing your block of ten ISBNs. But first, you have to nail down your book's title!

Congratulations, again, for taking these steps. We wish you the best of luck with your project and we are excited about seeing your book on the Internet or bookstore shelves soon! And if you have any questions along the way, don't be shy about contacting us. You're not alone! We wrote this book to help you and the help doesn't stop on the last page; we're available via e-mail or phone to answer your questions.

—Michele DeFilippo, owner, 1106 Design

Traditional Publisher Quality
For Independent Authors

Phoenix, Arizona
E-mail: md@1106design.com
https://1106design.com

Acknowledgments

'VE WORKED ON THOUSANDS of books, and thought I knew everything there was to know about producing a book quickly and efficiently. I knew the steps to follow, to be sure. Now I understand the emotions involved in birthing a book.

This book is small in pages, but it would not have been possible without the enormous effort and assistance of the talented group of experts at 1106 Design.

I would like to thank Laura, for invaluable copywriting and copyediting; Doran, for a spot-on title; Nathan, for a beautiful cover; Diane, for meticulous text design and typesetting; and last but not least, Ronda, for expert proofreading. I'm truly blessed to be surrounded by so many talented people.

To all the true professionals in the self-publishing community, who have the courage to stand for quality work. It's not easy to tell people what they need to hear, instead of what they want to hear. The education you so freely provide has been an inspiration to me, both professionally and personally, and it has made this book much better than it would otherwise be.

Last, but not least, to the clients of 1106 Design. You teach me more than you can imagine every day. Helping you realize your publishing dreams has been *my* dream come true.

About the Author

MICHELE DEFILIPPO owns 1106 Design, a Phoenix-based company that works with authors, publishers, business pros, coaches, consultants, speakers . . . anyone who wants a beautiful book, meticulously prepared to industry standards. 1106 Design offers top-quality cover design, beautifully designed and typeset interiors, manuscript editing, indexing, title consulting, author websites, and expert self-publishing advice. Unlike the one-size-fits-all solutions from "POD publishers," 1106 Design offers start-to-finish project management, customized to your specific needs, with hand-holding every step of the way. Please visit 1106design.com to view samples, read testimonials, and learn more, or contact Michele at md@1106design.com to discuss your book publishing goals.

www.ingramcontent.com/pod-product-compliance
Lightning Source LLC
Chambersburg PA
CBHW071838290426
44109CB00017B/1850